THE TRUTH ABOUT UNICORNS

by Molly Blaisdell   illustrated by Necdet Yilmaz

PICTURE WINDOW BOOKS
a capstone imprint

Thanks to our advisers for their expertise, research, and advice:

Elizabeth Tucker, PhD, Professor of English
Binghamton University, Binghamton, New York

Terry Flaherty, PhD, Professor of English
Minnesota State University, Mankato

Editor: Shelly Lyons
Designer: Lori Bye
Art Director: Nathan Gassman
Production Specialist: Jane Klenk
The illustrations in this book were created digitally.

Picture Window Books
151 Good Counsel Drive
P.O. Box 669
Mankato, MN 56002-0669
877-845-8392
www.capstonepub.com

All books published by Picture Window Books
are manufactured with paper containing at least
10 percent post-consumer waste.

Library of Congress Cataloging-in-Publication Data
Blaisdell, Molly, 1964-
  The truth about unicorns / by Molly Blaisdell ; illustrated by Necdet
Yilmaz.
      p. cm. — (Fairy-tale superstars)
  Includes index.
  ISBN 978-1-4048-5748-3 (library binding)
  1. Unicorns—Juvenile literature. I. Yilmaz, Necdet II. Title.
  GR830.U6B54 2010
  398.24'54—dc22
                                    2010000898

Printed in the United States of America in North Mankato, Minnesota.
102010   005987R

Are Unicorns Real?

Unicorns have shown up in stories for thousands of years. But has anyone ever seen one of these magical animals? Of course not! Unicorns aren't real.

What Do Unicorns Look Like?

The unicorn from European stories looks like a horse with a beard. It's coat is pearly white. The unicorn's long horn glows with light. The animal has blue eyes and a flowing mane. Its tail looks like a lion's tail.

flowing mane

blue eye

long, glowing horn

beard

lion's tail

horse's body

curved horn

lion's
head

Chinese symbol

deer's body

multicolored scale

The Chinese unicorn, or qilin (CHEE-lin), has a deer's
body. It has the head of a lion. Its horn is curved.
Sometimes the animal has two or three horns. Its
body is covered in scales. The scales can be red,
yellow, blue, white, and black. The qilin's back is
covered with symbols.

Unicorn Homes and Behavior

Stories show unicorns living in forests. A pond or stream is often nearby.

In tales, unicorns are signs of purity. They are powerful and noble. Stories also tell us unicorns are shy animals. But they will go near kind people. Unicorns are also quick and smart. They run away from hunters who might harm them.

Magical Horns

Throughout history, people have found "unicorn horns." But from what creatures did these horns really come? Sometimes the "unicorn horns" were actually the long, twisted teeth from whales called narwhals. When a narwhal dies, its long tooth might wash up on a beach. People have called the teeth unicorn horns.

Long ago, doctors thought unicorn horns healed the sick. They thought if you drank water from one, you would have a long life. Some people thought the horns would protect against poisons. For these reasons, people searched for unicorns and their horns.

Legend of the Unicorn

No one knows exactly when the legend of the unicorn began. One story started in India. People wrote about a strange unicorn. It had feet like an elephant and was the size of a horse. It had the tail of a goat and one bumpy black horn. But the animal wasn't a unicorn. It was a rhinoceros.

Another unicorn legend began in Tibet. The animal in this story is really an antelope. It has two straight horns. When seen from one side, the two horns appear to be one. From far away, the antelope looks like a unicorn.

Unicorn Folktales

A folktale from Europe tells the story of hunters who want a unicorn's magical horn. The hunters set a trap. They leave a beautiful young woman sitting in the forest. The unicorn is drawn to the woman's scent. The animal goes to her. The hunters catch the unicorn. The girl is sad until she sees something in the trees. The unicorn has escaped!

The Unicorn Tapestries

A similar unicorn story is told with pictures, not words. The pictures are woven into cloths called *The Unicorn Tapestries*. The tapestries were made in Europe more than 500 years ago.

In this picture story, hunters with dogs chase a unicorn. A woman tricks the unicorn to come to her. The hunters spear the unicorn. But the unicorn comes back to life.

The Chinese Unicorn

In a Chinese myth, the emperor of China wants to do something important for his people. He sits by a river to think. In the river, he sees a qilin. He sees colorful shapes on its back.

When the qilin leaves, the emperor traces the shapes he saw into the dirt. Suddenly the emperor knows these shapes could stand for words. The qilin has given him the start of the Chinese written language.

Unicorns Today

The legend of the unicorn is alive and well today. People still claim to see real unicorns. In 2008, a deer with a single horn in the middle of its forehead was found in Italy. Perhaps some old unicorn stories were based on this rare kind of deer.

In books and art today, unicorns are shown in bright colors, such as blue, green, and pink. Some of today's unicorns also have wings.

Modern Stories

People still love to read stories about unicorns. One popular story is *The Last Unicorn* by Peter S. Beagle. The story tells of an old unicorn that is told there are no more unicorns in the world. The unicorn, a magician, and a young woman work together to find the other unicorns. A scary creature called the Red Bull is holding the unicorns in its hideout. To set the unicorns free, the three friends drive the Red Bull into the sea.

In *Harry Potter and the Sorcerer's Stone*, by J.K. Rowling, Harry and another boy find unicorn blood in the forest. Later, they spy a dark figure drinking the blood of another unicorn. Harry soon learns the evil figure was drinking the unicorn's blood to stay alive.

Can You Find a Unicorn?

In books, movies, and art, unicorns are beautiful, brave, and smart. Though unicorns are make-believe, it's fun to think we may be able to see one hiding in a dark forest.

Legend Has It

- One Chinese myth suggests the unicorn helped create the world. Then the unicorn became the keeper of the forests.

- Long ago, if a carving of a unicorn head was hung above a door, it was a sign that a doctor worked there.

- English knights wear a special symbol called a coat of arms that sometimes features unicorns.

- *The Unicorn Tapestries* are still around today. They are on display at the Metropolitan Museum of Art in New York City.

Glossary

emperor—the male ruler of a country or group of countries

knight—a warrior who usually fights on horseback

legend—a story that seems to be true and is handed down from earlier times

myth—a story told by people in ancient times; a myth often tries to explain a natural event

noble—having or showing greatness of character

purity—freedom from evil

symbol—an object that stands for something else

tapestry—a heavy piece of cloth with pictures or patterns woven into it

Index

To Learn More

More Books to Read

Loewen, Nancy. *Once Upon a Time: Writing Your Own Fairy Tale.* Writer's Toolbox. Minneapolis: Picture Window Books, 2009.

Penner, Lucille Recht. *Unicorns.* New York: Random House, 2005.

Rake, Jody Sullivan. *Narwhal Whales Up Close.* Whales and Dolphins Up Close. Mankato, Minn.: Capstone Press, 2009.

Internet Sites

FactHound offers a safe, fun way to find Internet sites related to this book. All of the sites on FactHound have been researched by our staff.

Here's all you do:

Visit *www.facthound.com*

Type in this code: 9781404857483

Look for all the books in the Fairy-Tale Superstars series:

The Truth About Dragons

The Truth About Elves

The Truth About Fairies

The Truth About Princesses

The Truth About Trolls

The Truth About Unicorns